VIKINGS

VALERIE BODDEN

FIGHTERS
X
BOOKS

SCANDINAVIA

CREATIVE EDUCATION · CREATIVE PAPERBACKS

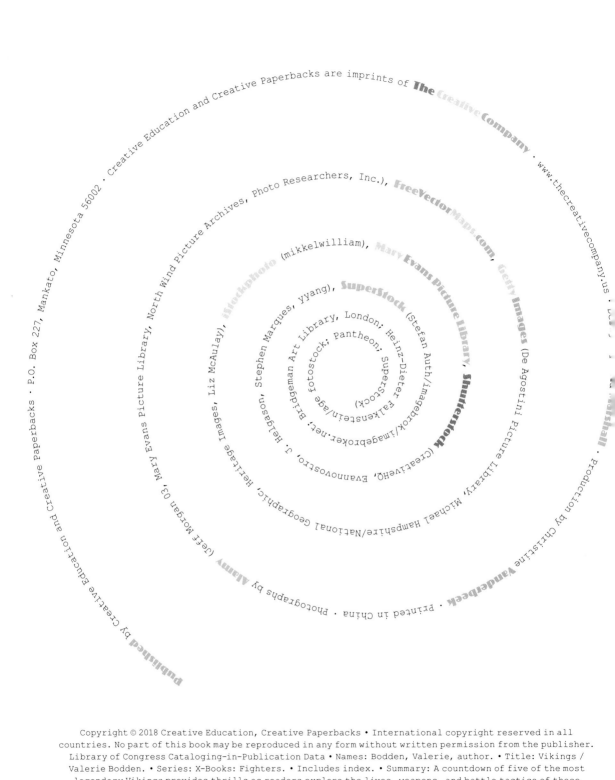

Published by Creative Education and Creative Paperbacks · P.O. Box 227, Mankato, Minnesota 56002 · Creative Education and Creative Paperbacks are imprints of The Creative Company · www.thecreativecompany.us · Production by Christine Vanderbeek · Printed in China · Photographs by Alamy (Jeff Morgan 03), Mary Evans Picture Library, North Wind Picture Library, Photo Researchers, Inc.), FreeVectorMaps.com, Getty Images (De Agostini Picture Library, Michael Hampshire/National Geographic, Heritage Images, Liz McAulay), iStockphoto (mikkelwilliam), Mary Evans Picture Library, Shutterstock (Stefan Auth/imagebroker/imagebroker.net; Evannovostro, CreativeHQ), SuperStock (Pantheon; SuperStock; fotostock; Bridgeman Art Library, London; Heinz-Dieter Falkenstein/age fotostock), J. Helgason, Stephen Marques, yyang)

VIK!NGS

CONTENTS

Xacting
FIGHTERS 5

Xciting
FACTS 28

Xtreme
TOP 5 VIKINGS

#5   **10**
#4   **16**
#3   **22**
#2   **26**
#1   **31**

FIGHTERS BOOKS

Xtensive
LEGACY 24

Xcessive
BATTLE 18

Xplosive
TACTICS 20

GLOSSARY

RESOURCES

INDEX 32

VIKING VOYAGES

Life on a Viking ship was dangerous. The northern seas were filled with icebergs. Sometimes it snowed. Fog made it easy to get lost. Strong storms wrecked ships. Many sailors drowned.

XACTING FIGHTERS

For almost 300 years, the sight of a Viking ship filled people with dread. These extreme fighters raided towns and villages. They were after **plunder**, slaves, and land.

VIKING PLUNDER gold, silver, iron, glass, jewels, statues, fabrics, jewelry, slaves

Viking Basics

The Vikings lived in Scandinavia. Scandinavia includes present-day Norway, Sweden, and Denmark. But the Vikings were not one group of people. Instead, they were made up of many different groups. Each group fought for its own chieftain.

The people of Scandinavia had a long history of building boats. In the A.D. 700s, they added sails to their ships. With the sails, they could travel farther. Soon, they discovered the wealth of other lands. They wanted that wealth. This led to the first Viking raids.

SCANDINAVIA

Many people who lived in Scandinavia were farmers. Warriors who went on raids were said to go "a-viking." They soon became known as Vikings.

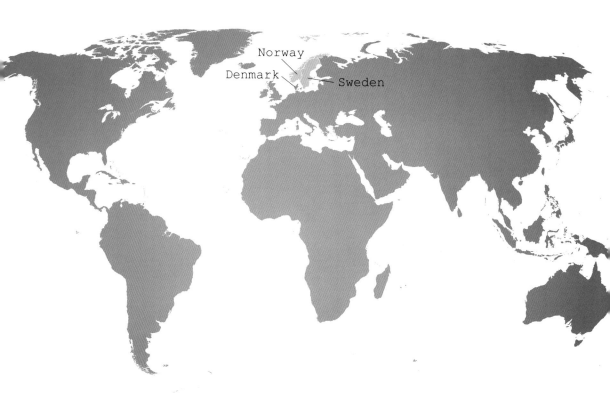

VIKING FARM ANIMALS cows, sheep, goats, pigs

VIKING CROPS barley, wheat, oats, onions, peas, beans

VIKINGS ATE A LOT OF FISH.

They hunted moose and reindeer, too.

VIKING RAIDS

Sometimes Vikings set up camps in other lands. From there, they raided farther inland. Sometimes they would take over the land and settle there.

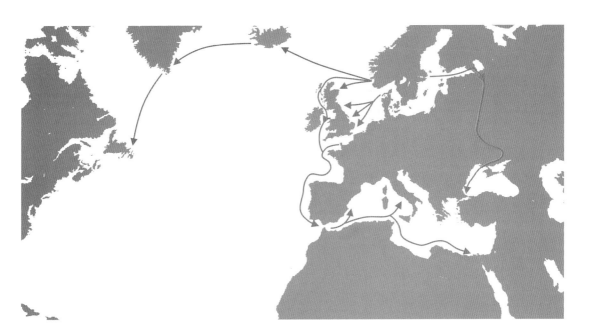

WHEN MEN WENT ON RAIDS,

their wives often took care of the farm.

MOST VIKING RAIDERS WERE YOUNG MEN.

Some women joined raids, too.

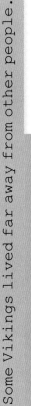

VIKING SETTLEMENT

Some Vikings lived far away from other people.

Others built small villages.

Each farm had a fence around it.

The Vikings' favorite targets were **monasteries** and trading towns. These places had many valuables. And they usually were not well guarded. Most Viking raids took place in Britain, France, and the Netherlands.

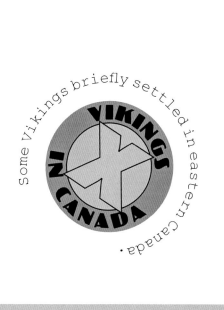

Some Vikings briefly settled in eastern Canada.

VIKINGS IN CANADA

VIKING BASICS FACT

e Vikings reached North America 500 years before Christopher Columbus.

TOP FIVE XTREME VIKINGS

Xtreme Viking #5

Erik Thorvaldsson is better known as Erik the Red, for his red hair. He was born in Norway. Later, he moved to Iceland. In A.D. 982, Erik was banned from Iceland for killing a man. He sailed west and discovered a new land. He called the land Greenland, even though it was icy. Erik became the leader of the Vikings in Greenland.

Poets called skalds told stories about the most heroic Vikings.

These stories were passed down over the years.

Life as a Viking

Most Viking families had a small farm. They lived in long, wooden homes called longhouses. A single home might include children, parents, and grandparents. The family lived at one end of the house. Animals were kept at the other end.

Viking boys learned to use weapons at a young age. They practiced battle skills by hunting. A Viking was taught to always be ready. He kept his weapons nearby, even when he was working in the field.

A Viking chieftain held feasts for his warriors. He won their loyalty by giving them gifts. He would give them arm rings made of gold or silver. Or he could give them weapons. Warriors were eager to fight for generous chieftains.

Vikings begin using sails

700s

Vikings take over Ireland entire

793

839

First Viking raid at a monastery in Britain

Vikings settle in Iceland and Greenland

900s

Vikings sail to North America

1000

Last major Viking battle

1066

Viking children climbed mountains and swam in cold water to get used to tough conditions.

Xtreme Viking #4

Freydis Eiriksdottir was the daughter of Erik Thorvaldsson. She was one of the few female Viking warriors. She joined a trip to Vinland (North America). As a Viking story says, Freydis killed the men in a rival crew before she returned home to Greenland. She did not want to share the wealth from what they had found.

XCESSIVE BATTLE

Vikings were not the best-armed warriors. But they learned to fight well with what they had. By far, their most important piece of equipment was the longship.

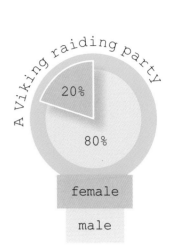

A Viking raiding party

20%

80%

female

male

VIKING WEAPONS FACT

Viking warriors named their swords after fierce animals.

They thought this made the swords strong.

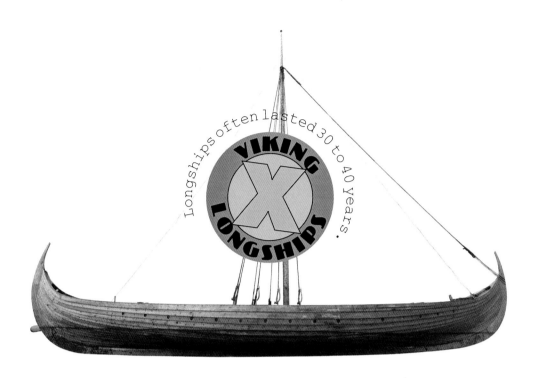

Longships often lasted 30 to 40 years.

VIKING LONGSHIPS

Viking Ships & Weapons

Viking ships were known as longships. Longships were 60 to 120 feet (18.3–36.6 m) long. Both the front and the back of the ship were pointed. This allowed sailors to change direction without turning the ship around. All Viking ships had a shallow draft. Because not much of the ship was underwater, it could go into shallow rivers. It could be pulled onto beaches, too.

Longships had one large, square sail. They had oars, too. Oars were used when there was no wind. They were also used to travel up rivers.

Swords were expensive weapons. Only a few warriors could afford them. Most Viking warriors carried a spear. Vikings wielded axes, too. Some Vikings used a bow and arrows in battle. Warriors carried round shields made of wood and leather to protect against enemy weapons.

XPLOSIVE TACTICS

Vikings liked to make surprise attacks. They often attacked on Sundays or holidays. They knew people would be in churches. The people would not be prepared to fight back.

XPLOSIVE TACTICS FACT

Viking shields could be hung over the back by a strap. This freed both hands for fighting.

Berserkers were the fiercest Viking warriors. They did not wear any armor. These fighters whirled and danced before a fight. Then they rushed into battle. Their behavior scared opponents.

Viking ships sailed toward the shore quickly. The
warriors stormed into a town. They grabbed gold,
jewelry, and other treasures. They kidnapped people
to be sold as slaves.

 The Vikings sometimes met their enemies on the
battlefield. A Viking battle started with the two sides
lined up across from each other. The men at the front
knelt. They held their shields in front of them to form
a wall. Both sides hurled rocks and spears. They shot
arrows, too. Then the armies advanced. The men fought
one-on-one with swords and spears. Sometimes they
dropped their weapons and wrestled.

3

TOP FIVE XTREME VIKINGS

Xtreme Viking #3

Cnut the Great's father was the king of Denmark. After his father's death in 1016, Cnut invaded England. He defeated the English king. Then he took the throne for himself. Later, he became king of Denmark, Norway, and parts of Sweden, too. Cnut's rule was largely peaceful. He held power until his death in 1035.

XTENSIVE LEGACY

Viking attacks slowed in the 1000s. By then, powerful Viking kings had taken control of Scandinavia. There were fewer chieftains to fight each other.

Cnut the Great, Viking king

Viking Legacy

Monasteries and towns became better at fighting off the Vikings. The last Viking battle took place in 1066. The Viking king Harald Hardrada was defeated in England. After that, Viking raids stopped.

Today, the Vikings are remembered through movies and books. People in some places hold Viking fairs and festivals. They build copies of Viking ships. Sports teams such as the Minnesota Vikings use Viking symbols as their mascot. The age of the Vikings may be over, but their legacy lives on.

VIKING GODS		
Odin	poetry, magic, war
Thor	storms, strength, destruction
Njord	sailing, hunting
Freyja	love

Much of what is known about Vikings comes from accounts written by victims of their violence. But today, people also point out the positive parts of Viking culture. The Vikings were not only warriors. They were also traders, explorers, and craftsmen. Their travels brought new goods to northern Europe. Their ships advanced sailing technology. They changed history.

XTENSIVE LEGACY FACT

In 2007, builders made a longship using Viking tools.

They sailed it 1,000 miles (1,609 km).

25

Xtreme Viking #2

Leif Eriksson was the son of Erik Thorvaldsson. He was born in Iceland around A.D. 970. He later moved to Greenland. There, he heard stories of lands to the west. Leif put together a group to explore this land. He became the first European to reach North America. He set up a camp there. He cut down trees and took the wood back to Greenland. Other Vikings settled briefly in North America.

XCITING FACTS

Viking ships sailed in fleets, or groups, of 3 to 100 ships.

When a Viking boy was around 12 years old, he could go on his first raid

Viking chieftains were buried in longships.
Their weapons were buried with them.

For battle, some wealthy Vikings wore a chain mail shirt made of small
linked metal rings.

Viking spears were six to nine feet (1.8–2.7 m) long.
Each spear had a two-foot (0.6 m) blade.

Viking swords were double-edged.
This means both sides of the blade were sharp.

A boat oar could be used to knock an enemy over the head.

Small Viking longships had 26 oars. The biggest ships had up to 68 oar

Vikings slept in sealskin sleeping bags on the deck of their longsh

Some towns gave the Vikings treasures
to keep the warriors from attacking.

For sea battles, the Vikings tied their ships together. Then they
boarded the enemy's ships to fight.

The Vikings wrote with symbols called runes.

A Viking ship could sail at speeds of 17 miles (27.4 km) per hour.

Longships are sometimes

alled dragonships.

Many had carved dragons on the front.

Xtreme Viking #1

Harald Hardrada is often called the last Viking. He was born in Norway in 1015. He fought for his half-brother, the **exiled** king of Norway. When his brother was killed, Harald ran away. He spent time fighting for the **Byzantine Empire**. This made him a wealthy military commander. When he returned home, he became the king of Norway. In 1066, he was killed in a battle against England.

GLOSSARY

Byzantine Empire – an empire that ruled much of southeastern Europe and western Asia from A.D. 395 to 1453

exiled – forced to live away from one's country

monasteries – places where monks (a religious group of men who agree to remain poor and unmarried) live

plunder – goods stolen by force

RESOURCES

Fitzhugh, William, and Elisabeth Ward, eds. *Vikings: The North Atlantic Saga*. Washington, D.C.: Smithsonian Institution Press, 2000.

Hall, Richard. *The World of the Vikings*. New York: Thames & Hudson, 2007.

Williams, Gareth, Peter Pentz, and Matthias Wemhoff, eds. *Vikings: Life and Legend*. Ithaca, N.Y.: Cornell University Press, 2014.

Winroth, Anders. *The Age of the Vikings*. Princeton, N.J.: Princeton University Press, 2014.

INDEX

chieftains and kings 5, 12, 22, 24, 28, 31

famous Vikings 10, 11, 16, 22, 24, 26, 31

farming 6, 7, 8, 12

fighting tactics 20, 21, 28

Greenland 10, 13, 16, 26

Iceland 10, 13, 26

legacy 11, 24, 25

North America 9, 13, 16, 26

plundering and raids 5, 6, 7, 8, 12, 21, 22, 24, 28

Scandinavia 5, 6, 10, 22, 24, 31

ships 4, 5, 18, 19, 21, 24, 25, 28

Viking culture 5, 6, 7, 8, 12, 15, 25, 28

"viking" meaning 6

weapons 12, 18, 19, 21, 28

Viking axes had long handles and sharp, wide heads made of iron.